Successful
Negotiating

If you want to know how...

Create Great Spreadsheets
*How to set up and use spreadsheets for business
and personal finance*

80/20 Management
Work smarter, not harder, and quadruple your results

Leading Teams
Delivering results through teamworking

The Management Speaker's Sourcebook
How to give your presentation confidently and with style

100 Ways to Make Your Business a Success
A small business resource book

howtobooks

Please send for a free copy of the latest catalogue:

How To Books
3 Newtec Place, Magdalen Road,
Oxford OX4 1RE, United Kingdom
info@howtobooks.co.uk
www.howtobooks.co.uk

Business Essentials

Successful Negotiating

Getting what you want in the best way possible

Patrick Forsyth

howto books

Published by How To Books Ltd,
3 Newtec Place, Magdalen Road,
Oxford OX4 1RE. United Kingdom.
Tel: (01865) 793806. Fax: (01865) 248780.
info@howtobooks.co.uk
www.howtobooks.co.uk

First published 2002
Reprinted 2004

British Library Cataloguing in Publication Data.
A catalogue record for this book is available from
the British Library.

Cover design by Baseline Arts Ltd, Oxford
Produced for How To Books by Deer Park Productions
Typeset by PDQ Typesetting, Newcastle-under-Lyme, Staffs.
Printed and bound by Bell & Bain Ltd, Glasgow

NOTE: The material contained in this book is set out in good faith for
general guidance and no liability can be accepted for loss or expense
incurred as a result of relying in particular circumstances on statements
made in the book. Laws and regulations are complex and liable to change,
and readers should check the current position with the relevant authorities
before making personal arrangements.

Contents

Preface

If you want a guinea pig, then you start by asking for a pony

Annabel, aged 6 (quoted in an Internet newsletter)

The above quotation is a delight. It is also indicative of wisdom way beyond the speaker's age, and of an apparently inherent understanding of a core principle of the process of negotiation. Doubtless Annabel has more to learn, but she is off to a good start.

Negotiation may seem, at first sight, like something that other people do. High-powered business people, politicians and union leaders negotiate. So they do. But, put more simply they are *bargaining,* and all of us do that. When we do, and do so successfully, we can smooth relations, save money, time, aggravation and face in many different situations. The negotiating process involves balancing matters between two parties so that you not only get what you want (that is persuade – see the guide *Anyone Can Sell* by Rob Young, also an *Essentials* paperback), but get what you want in the best possible way. It is the art of concluding a deal, and the arrangement of all the elements that constitute that deal; for instance, the terms and conditions in some business deals. It is a form of communication and, as such, is an interactive process. There is thus no one right approach, though there are certainly principles that form the basis of any success. What works for one situation may not be right for another, but what we find does work will probably help the next time we are in similar circumstances.

This short book sets out the essentials – what really matters – about the process. It reviews the core techniques and approaches that provide a basis for undertaking negotiation, and aims to make them understandable and manageable. Given that this is a skill that you can spend a lifetime develop-ing, it also provides a basis from which you can fine-tune in the future to sharpen your skills further.

Patrick Forsyth

1 · Getting to Grips with the Process

Understanding the overall way in which negotiation works is the first step to being able to undertake it.

In this Chapter:

Negotiating can be a complex process, but the elements that make it up are essentially straightforward. The complexity is largely in the orchestration of the various elements into a cohesive and fluent conversation. If such orchestration is to be achieved successfully then each aspect of the process must be addressed in turn, and what is only a form of communication – though certainly a special one – must be made to work.

Communication is not the easiest thing in the world. How often do you hear, or are you involved in, the results of confused communication? In offices, and homes too, around the world phrases such as – *but I thought you meant*...and *that's not what you said* – are all too common. Negotiation cannot work unless communication is clear. What is more, it normally occurs in parallel with persuasion. Persuasion seeks to obtain agreement, negotiation organises that agreement into a form where the arrangement of the details is agreed; both are separate topics worth some separate study if you are to negotiate successfully.

Further, there is an adversarial aspect to negotiation. Both parties want to win. One of the tricks of successful negotiation, therefore, is for it to end with both sides feeling they have done well – the so-called 'win–win' outcome. The adversarial aspect must be controlled or conversations will deteriorate into slanging matches and, at worst, any sort of agreement will be forfeit. So your approach to negotiating needs to see it as a two-way process; it is not a question of steamrollering your 'opponent' but of give and take with them. Of course both parties want to create an edge for themselves, and each has their own objectives; getting close to what you want without upsetting the whole fabric of the process is the skill you need to develop.

It is achieving what you want yet making the process acceptable that is key. Remember the old saying: poker playing is not to be learnt in one evening.

1 · DEFINING THE PROCESS

There is more to negotiating than may at first meet the eye. Consider what negotiation is not. It is not simply stating a grievance. Imagine the toaster has come back from the menders and is still doing a good impression of a crematorium. It would be most people's instinct to complain, but often without proposing a remedy. At best, complaints produce apologies. At worst, they produce arguments in which threats produce counter-threats, and even an impasse.

All too often communication can end up this way. It starts with a complaint: 'Productivity in your department is dropping', 'Sales results are below target', and deteriorates into an argument: 'No, it's not', 'There are good reasons for that' and so on.

What you really want in such circumstances is action. You have to suggest, or prompt, a proposal: something that will put things right. Arguments cannot be negotiated, only proposals can. This, in turn, demands that emotions are kept under control. Negotiation is a delicate process, which needs thinking about carefully — both before and during it.

■ **Win–win dealing.** It is inherent to the process of negotiation that both the parties involved end up feeling satisfied that an appropriate deal has been struck. It may not be exactly the result they hoped for, but it is one they can realistically agree to. It is this outcome that gives rise to the description of a win–win negotiating situation. Some individuals feel they must win every point, deliberately creating a win–lose approach. Negotiation is, however, a process of some give and take, and if both parties accept this then a win–win approach is more likely to achieve a productive conclusion.

■ **Looking at the implications.** Some examples of the implications of win-win negotiation are shown below.

1. The emphasis should be on seeking common ground, rather than fighting for your way on everything.

2. Relate to the other party and their concerns, rather than just objecting to them.

3. Be ready to compromise, at least to some degree, rather than remain inflexible.

4. Discussion must accommodate to-and-fro debate, rather than insist on a rigid agenda.

5. Discussion should include questioning – and thus listening – rather than just giving statements of your case.

6. Appropriate information should be disclosed, rather than maintaining total secretiveness.

7. Building relationships rather than bad feelings between parties is important.

8. The aim is agreement not stalemate.

A win–win conclusion should normally be your aim.

> *Always keep in mind: negotiation is the process of identifying, arranging and agreeing the terms and conditions, whatever they may be, of a deal.*

- **Complexities demand care.** Negotiation is a complex process. Several elements need to be borne in mind if the process is to move along satisfactorily.

Remember that persuasive communication starts the process. This is where one party puts across their case and the other begins, in their own mind, to accept it. As agreement in principle begins to emerge the question switches from 'Will this person agree?' to 'On what basis will they agree?' Each party is then concerned that every detail making up the deal will suit them as much as possible. It may be impossible for both to be satisfied one hundred per cent on every factor – indeed this will probably not be so – but the balance must be right.

2 · **TRADING AND USING VARIABLES**

The different factors that are the raw material of negotiation are called **variables**. They may indeed be many and various, and this fact contributes to the overall complexity of the negotiation process. An everyday example will illustrate the point.

Imagine you are going to make some major household purchase: a refrigerator, perhaps. Which model you buy, and from where, will depend on a number of factors – perhaps a surprisingly large number. There is price, of course. But there are also factors about the fridge itself: the star rating of its freezer unit, the size, number and arrangements of shelves, bottle-holding capacity, the colour, which way the door opens and so on. There may be other, less obvious factors. How much does it cost to run? Will they deliver it, by when and with what certainty? Will they carry it up to a third-floor apartment? What payment terms are available? What guarantee and service arrangements apply? You can no doubt think of more.

This kind of purchase may consist only of checking and considering such factors and then making a decision, but some of the factors may not be fixed. Some will be offered – or not – by the shop, others have to be suggested and negotiated. You only get certain things included in the deal when they have been raised, discussed and agreed. Once this process is involved then balance is necessary. Both parties may need to give as well as take.

- You agree to delay delivery by two weeks, and they will deliver free of charge when they have a van coming your way.

- They agree to knock, say, ten per cent off the price if you agree to pay cash, and so on.

In other words you 'trade' variables. You swap aspects of them to balance and re-balance the deal. Such trading may use all or part of a variable: for instance, you might agree to collect the fridge, foregoing any kind of delivery, but in return for more discount. The techniques of trading variables will be investigated further as we progress.

■ **Evaluating the raw materials of negotiation.** Variables are the raw materials of negotiation. Each one has a scale of possible decisions on which we must settle and agree. For example:

– Discount: none or fifty per cent.
– Delivery: this afternoon, at exactly 3pm, this week, next week, sometime. . .

There are often many variables; we need a clear idea of what position on the scale is likely to be acceptable to us, and the relative importance of different ones.

The more variables there are, and the harder they are to prioritise, the more complex the negotiation becomes.

The human interactions inherent in the process complicate the negotiation.

■ **Increasing success.** If we are not careful, we may look back after a meeting and conclude we lost out. Perhaps we failed to recognise the need for negotiation. If such an under-estimate is made, then any transaction will be handled inade-quately and the end result is likely to be a bad deal.

For example, an administration manager may telephone a supplier to complain about an incorrectly completed service on a company car. A complaint may produce no more than an apology. If the manager wants something done about it he or she must suggest a remedy: maybe balancing the inconveni-ence of the car going back with the seriousness of the fault and the option of leaving it until the next service.

There are many different approaches possible here, and very different arrangements may result from them. If you see something as negotiation, but go at it like 'a bull at a gate', or focus exclusively on one element or allow the transaction to develop into an argument, you are unlikely to achieve what you want.

■ **Knowing the fundamentals of success.** Success in negotiation rests on three interrelated fundamentals:

1. *What you do*. The techniques and processes of all sorts that are involved.

2. *How you go about it*. The manner you employ and the effects this has on those with whom you negotiate.

3. *Preparation*. The first two fundamentals are both dependent on this. Given the complexities already mentioned, preparing for negotiation is no more than common sense. Yet it is easier said than done. Probably more negotiators fail to reach the best arrangement for want of adequate preparation than for any other reason. This links to two further important points.

Working at success is fundamental. It was Vidal Sassoon who said 'The only place where success comes before work is in the dictionary.' Success in negotiation, as in so much else in life, does not just happen. People with good skills in this area tend to make it look easy. A good cook or a skilful public speaker make what they do seem effortless, but this does not mean that a good deal of preparation has not been necessary for this impression to be given.

Accepting that some preparation is always necessary, however long or short the process may need to be, is the first step to success.

Note, and this may be a compensation if preparation sounds like a bit of a chore, that sound preparation can give you your first 'edge' in negotiation. It can act, almost regardless of other factors, to give you a head start in comparison with another person, particularly one who has skimped in this area.

Such an edge is often vital. In many kinds of negotiation no quarter is given. Think of the vehemence of some international negotiations between nations, or of certain wage-bargaining situations. A great deal may hang on the outcome and the negotiator needs to have on their side every trick of the trade in order to create an edge.

The following story (from my book *Everything You Need to Know About Marketing* Kogan Page) takes sales situations as its base and reinforces the need for creating as much of an edge as possible.

It is any buyer's job to get the best possible deal for their organisation. That is what they are paid for; they are not actually on the sales people's side, and will attempt to get the better of them in any way they can, especially with regard to price.

This is well illustrated by the apocryphal story of the fairground strongman. During his act he took an orange, put it in the crook of his arm and, bending his arm, squeezed the juice out. He then challenged anyone in the audience to squeeze out any more, offering a cash prize to anyone who could successfully squeeze out even one more drop.

After many had tried unsuccessfully, one apparently unlikely candidate came forward. He squeezed and squeezed, and finally out came just a couple more drops. The strongman was amazed and, seeking to explain how it was possible, asked as he paid up what the man did for a living. 'I'm a buyer with Ford Motor Company.'

Buyers are not really like this; they are worse.

Such people really are there in part to apply pressure to get the best deal. And it is not just buyers in major companies, or indeed buyers in general, who do this. It could be anyone you negotiate with. They will be intent on fighting their corner, meeting their objectives, financial or otherwise, and will do their best for their position – not yours. The next question concerns how to go about it.

Preparing and preparing sufficiently thoroughly to influence what you do, is not just worthwhile, it can make the difference between success and failure.

3 · **PREPARING TO NEGOTIATE**

Do you think of yourself as inexperienced at – even wary of – the process of negotiation? This is, at least in part, only because you are ill prepared for doing it. Being well prepared breeds confidence. Confidence allows the process to be better managed than an ad hoc approach ever will be. In addition, others will read the fact of your appearing confident as competence; the way we appear is very important, as we will explore later.

Preparation may constitute just a few moments' thought prior to the start of a conversation. It may be a few minutes, or an hour or two of homework. Or it may mean sitting round the table with colleagues, thrashing out the best way forward and sometimes even rehearsing what will be done.

Whatever scale of preparation circumstances dictate, it must always take place.

4 · **RELATING TO OTHERS**

Preparation cannot be done in a vacuum. You need to consider both the other people involved and your own position.

The first stage of preparation is to consider the person (or people) with whom you must negotiate and, if appropriate, the organisation they represent. Negotiation may take place with all sorts of people: customers, suppliers, business colleagues (boss, subordinates) and you may or may not know them personally.

Questions need to be answered about such people, for example:

■ What role and/or intentions do they have?

■ What needs (subjective and objective) do they have? What problems will they raise?

■ What objections will they raise?

■ Can they decide things, or must they consult with someone else?

Each situation will raise different issues, but the principle of thinking through how people may handle something is similar in each case. Do not overlook this, or assume familiarity makes it unnecessary.

Even with people you know and deal with regularly, such analysis may pay dividends.

Now consider an example. Imagine you are making arrangements with the banquet manager at a hotel or conference centre for the annual company general meeting. You want it to go well. You want the arrangements to be appropriate. You want it to be memorable. The banquet manager wants it to go well too, of course, but he is also concerned that it should fit in with other functions, be easy to staff and be profitable.

For your part you must be sure the banquet manager has sufficient authority to make the arrangements you want, that he is professional, knowledgeable, and that what he says will be possible will prove to be so on the day.

Suppose he suggests a combination of rooms A and B. You feel B and C would suit better. Is his suggestion based on how your group will best be accommodated, or to allow him to fit the local football club in room C? And do you want them next door anyway?

As each element such as cost and catering is discussed and various options reviewed, your knowledge of the banquet manager and his intentions will allow you to negotiate more successfully than if you knew nothing. You may never have met him before, but some consideration of what he is likely to be feeling and planning will always help. This is true of whomever you deal with.

Considering your own position is also vital. How you are seen is important, too. People will respect you more if they feel you appear professional, or expert, if you clearly have the authority to negotiate and if you appear prepared, confident and in charge.

You may never be quite as close to this ideal as you would like, but often the other person has no way of knowing this, and 'appear' is indeed the right word. Some people seem to have the confidence to tell you black is white and make you believe it. The exception to this is appearing to be prepared. You must, as has been said, actually *be* prepared, though it does no harm to appear even better prepared than you actually are. All this means it is essential to think about matters thoroughly.

5 · SETTING CLEAR OBJECTIVES

Having objectives firmly in mind — knowing exactly what you are trying to achieve — is key. But surely there is no problem in making them clear? Let us pick up the earlier example of the company annual meeting. The objectives for the annual company meeting were effectively stated as being that it should be:

- successful (meeting its specific objectives)
- felt by everyone to be appropriate in style and purpose
- memorable: setting the scene for the year to come.

But there is more to consider. What about cost? Are these objectives regardless of cost or do they have to be achieved within a budget? What about the provision of equipment and visual aids? This introduces another area of variables, and another scale against which matters must be judged and settled.

The answer might be that the objectives can certainly not be considered regardless of cost, but that the budget must be realistic if what is wanted is to be achieved well. Similarly, if visual aids are vital, the date of the meeting itself could be changed to secure a larger and better-equipped meeting room, where the right equipment can be easily accommo- dated and a more professional show can be put on.

You need to identify and set specific (and thus measurable) objectives.

Objectives, an old maxim says, should be SMART: Specific, Measurable, Achievable, Realistic and Timed.

You need to have your priorities clear, and clearly related to what variables are involved, and understand your attitude to each. For example, are there some variables about which you are prepared to compromise? If so, how far are you prepared to go? And are there others about which you intend to be immovable?

Another key factor is **timing**.

Are you intent on achieving everything at once, in one meeting? Or is there a long-term strategy involved? The reason for thinking through what your objectives are is not academic; your clarity and assurance about them help you conduct the kind of meeting that will enable you reach them.

> *With negotiation, as with most things, 'ready, aim, fire' is always likely to be the best order in which to proceed!*

6 · STRUCTURING THE MEETING

The thinking described above is designed to influence the way a meeting works. In fact, your preparation should anticipate something of all the factors that make up the complexities of negotiation (thus we return to it in the last chapter in a summary).

Preparation also includes matters relevant to the message with which the negotiation is bound up. For example, you may need to think how arguments can be justified as your point of view is explained. This goes back to general communication and its focus; for example, making things persuasive.

As we have seen, the variable factors of negotiation are, in effect, traded; this can mean that some elements of the variables are used as concessions. You may find the jargon here confusing, as some people use 'variable' and 'concession' almost interchangeably. In fact, while all variables may be traded, not all may be used as concessions in the sense of giving something away. But here the only point to make is that you will handle this give-and-take process much better if you have thought through some of the options.

Continuing the example of the company annual meeting, the organiser might deal with the banquet manager thus: 'If we start an hour later, and choose an alternative menu, can we have the larger room at the same cost?'

Here three elements, timing, menu and room options, are being used together in relation to overall cost – and within a single sentence. Such a discussion can get very much more complicated.

■ **Maintaining structure in the meeting.** Structure means the shape and to some extent the style of the meeting. Structure encompasses everything that will avoid any sort of muddle.

  – What do you envisage doing?
  – What will you aim to do first, second and third?

Account needs to be taken of likely timing. For example, do you have one hour, several hours, or must everything be agreed more promptly? Your order of sequence and priority must fit within the duration of the meeting. You will need to be very clear which are primary and which are secondary matters. If time runs short you do not want to find you have omitted anything of primary concern.

A well-written report has a beginning, a middle and end; so does a good presentation. Both may require a detailed structure within each main segment, however, and a negotiation meeting is similar.

You also need to anticipate the tone of the meeting. As well as what you want to do, how do you want it to go in terms of manner and feeling?

For example, there may be stages at which you wish to be seen as particularly reasonable, or the opposite, and stages when you need to come over with some real clout.

What kind of personal profile do you wish to project? Make sure that your negotiating role is not in conflict with this. One should enhance the other.

Remaining flexible during preparation is important; don't cast it in tablets of stone. You can never know for sure what the other party will do, but a clear plan still helps. It sets out your intention: what you would like to do.

Think of your plan as a route map, not a straitjacket. Good planning should not prevent you being flexible and responding to circumstances. Indeed it makes it easier to do so. A route map does not prevent you from changing your route if you unexpectedly find road works in the way. Indeed it helps you both to divert *and* get back on track.

Preparation is the foundation of successful negotiation.

Negotiation does not just happen, nor does the detail of how the meeting needs to progress. As we review the conduct of negotiation, both the shape of the meeting and the detail within that shape will become clearer.

IN SUMMARY

- Keep the win–win nature of negotiation in mind.

- Identify and organise the variables that you will trade at the meeting.

- Prepare – think through the *what* and *how* of the meeting.

- Resolve to keep the other party in mind throughout the process.

- Set clear objectives.

- Think about the structure of the negotiation; it will help you manage the process.

2 · Negotiating Tactics

To deploy the techniques successfully you must also manage the process.

In this Chapter:

The complexities of negotiation put a high premium on managing the meeting effectively. During the process two separate factors are in train together. First, the process itself and the deployment of the tactics of negotiation, and secondly, the interpersonal behaviour which accompanies them.

Both are important – separately and as they work together.

In order to build up a clear picture of the process, we leave the interpersonal behaviour on one side for the moment and deal specifically with the tactical basis for negotiation.

1 · USING VARIABLES

It is a fundamental necessity for the successful negotiator to have a sound knowledge of all the variables, and their possible use in trading. You must:

- see variables in the round in order to prepare an opening strategy — a starting point for discussion

- decide how the variables can be used to trade; assess their respective worth

- continue to search throughout the negotiation for other factors that might be used as variables.

Occasionally one party in negotiation holds all the cards and the result may be in little doubt. More often the situation is not a foregone conclusion; the balance might go either way and things start apparently on a flat field, but many arrangements are possible. Just how everything is done is a deciding factor.

> *Keep in mind that techniques should be used but not advertised. As Duc de la Rochefoucauld said: 'The height of cleverness is to be able to conceal it'.*

2 · THE POWER YOU BRING TO THE TABLE

Before getting into more detail about the use of variables we must consider what brings power to our discussions.

What acts to swing the balance? It is the power to negotiate that both sides bring to the table. Everyone hopes to have the balance of power. It is something to consider in your planning and certainly something to be realistic about; a major mistake for negotiators is to over- or under-estimate the power held either by themselves or by their opposite number.

The word power is used here in a very specific manner. Nego-tiators mean a number of things by it. The main power factors are as follows.

■ **Using specific variables**. The most obvious sources of power are the specific variables that are most important to a particular negotiation. These can be almost anything, from major matters like financial arrangements including price, dis-counts and payment terms, to a plethora of others.

They can be either tangible or intangible, and usually some of both sorts are involved. This is an area where feeling is as important as substance. For instance, aspects of the company meeting mentioned earlier may well be subjective: how will the way it is organised affect the participants?

- **Using a promise of reward**. This term describes something you can offer that the other party definitely wants, so that they are inclined to listen. The banquet manager in the example earlier wants the business, giving one major element of power to the event organiser. There is a corresponding negative side to this that is identified next.

- **Using a threat of punishment**. This is where there is an apparent intention not to give something that the other party wants. Thus, if the banquet manager refuses to agree some factor important to the organiser, he wields power; this may be increased if the organiser knows it is short notice and he is unlikely to get availability and a better deal elsewhere.

- **Using legitimacy**. Legitimacy means the factual evidence. It can swing the balance without much argument: for example, if the event organiser shows a written quote from another venue then, provided it compares like with like, its presence influences both parties.

- **Using bogeys**. Bogeys are factors used specifically to produce an edge. They may not stand up to great examination,
  but in the throes of a meeting can be used to good effect.
  For example, saying 'My chairman is insistent upon . . .' may la-
  bel a particular point as unalterable – while the truth of the
  matter may be unclear. Bogeys may be factors used only for
  what they can achieve, or may be factors that are actually of
  some importance, but which are given artificial weight in the
  hopes of their securing an edge.

- **Showing confidence**. Confidence comes in part from preparation. It has a lot to do with the human and behavioural
  aspects of negotiation, which are explored later. It is harder
  to deal with someone who appears very confident, and who
  seems to have every reason to be so. Clearly, you want to feel
  that the one with the most justifiable confidence is you, and
  work in every way possible to achieve this.

As you think through what the bargaining variables are, try to
assess the power they give you. This is not simply a numbers
game. Having a larger number of variables, while undeniably

useful, may not itself guarantee more negotiating power. Some variables may be lightweight and make little difference; others may be particularly telling and powerful.

The net effect of all the elements that contribute to your coming to the negotiating table in a position of some power is important to the outcome. This is an area to consider carefully.

> *The detail here is important: just one more thing well considered could increase your power over a threshold that impacts the whole meeting and influences the outcome significantly.*

Categorising variables

Negotiating variables differ both in nature and potential. Similarly, their roles in trading may vary. Linking them to your plan and objectives will show you their potential role in the subsequent proceedings.

Three types of variable are usually highlighted:

■ the *must haves*: those factors you feel you must take from the negotiation if the deal is to be at all acceptable to you

■ the *ideals*: those factors which you would like to achieve, and which would constitute the ideal deal. Realistically these must include factors around which you are prepared to make some compromise

■ the *loss leaders*: loss leaders take their name from products sold in stores at nil or negative profit margins simply to attract buyers; the buyers then create profit by purchasing other products on their visit. In negotiation we mean those aspects we are really prepared to trade with, even if we would prefer not to, in order to finalise. You must have some things in this category.

Trading is fundamental to negotiation. There is, in a way, a ritual to be completed, and without that no progress is possible. If all you do is state an unchangeable position and refuse to move, the outcome may be permanent stalemate.

So too is how you organise yourself to do it: categorising in the way discussed makes the whole process more precise and manageable.

Some say this was what caused Sir Edward Heath's downfall as Prime Minister years ago; during the miners' strike he did just this. Believing that his first offer could not, by definition, be his last, the miners dug in their heels. There was effectively no negotiation, and the government toppled.

With a view in mind of what you have to work with, we can now turn to the tactical principles that will help you conduct an effective meeting.

3 · THE KEY TACTICAL PRINCIPLES

There are four guiding principles which combine to help the successful management of negotiations.

■ **Setting your sights high**. 'Faint heart never won fair lady' says an old saying. Always aim high. It is important to aim for the top, for the best deal you can imagine, because it is always easier to manage the process from this starting point. You can always trade down; indeed you may often have to do so, but it is more difficult, indeed often impossible, to trade up having originally stated lower intentions. It is especially difficult to change tactics and trade up well into the meeting. It is for this reason that having a clear view of the variables – the must haves and so on detailed above – is so useful. You may not always achieve exactly what you want, but the chances of getting close are most likely with this approach.

■ **Finding out the other person's full intentions**. Think of the other person in the same way as you think of yourself. They too have a shopping list of what they want to do. The better your information about what this is, the better you will be able to operate. It is easy to make superficial judgements. There may well be some obvious things they are after, but other factors matter too, as do their priorities. The more complete your picture the better. Information may come from:

– prior preparation
– knowledge or experience of the person or situation, or ones like them
– questions asked as an integral, perhaps early, part of the negotiation meeting.

Infer sensibly by all means, but be wary of making unwarranted assumptions as this can lead you on false trails if you are wrong. It is all too easy to come out of a meeting that has not gone so well, saying 'but it seemed so obvious . . .' Your thinking this may have been the other's exact intention; you were led where they wanted you to go.

■ **Keeping all the factors in mind**. As the picture builds up, the complexities grow. It is easy as you plan ahead to forget some of the issues you need to keep in mind. You need to keep a clear head, to make notes, think and recap as necessary if each step forward is going to work.

- **Keeping a look out for further variables**. You need to remain flexible. Avoid getting locked in to previous plans; remember planning is only a guide. The good negotiator is quick on their feet. Sometimes what happens is very much along the lines you expect, but some fine-tuning is always necessary — and sometimes a great deal needs to be done.

The saying that 'everything is negotiable' can be true. Certainly something that has been described as fixed may suddenly come into play. There is merit in remaining open minded to such possibilities and, where appropriate, taking the initiative.

> *A key way of doing this is to float alternatives using questions that start 'What if . . .'. This extends consideration but does not commit you to agreement.*

4 · MANAGING THE PROCESS

The process of negotiation assumes what is called a point of balance. It is inherent in the process that while participants start far apart on the scale of possibilities for agreement, they will settle on something they can both relate to as a reasonable deal.

The point of balance on which agreement is struck is not, of course, usually spot on the centre. A range of solutions is possible around the middle point. Similarly the furthest – or most extreme – points from the centre are usually quickly recognised by both parties as unrealistic goals and only relevant as starting points. Movement along the scale is what characterises a discussion as negotiating. A good analogy is a child's see-saw. The job of negotiating is to move things along its length. Realistically we will not achieve something that is at the ends (where the children sit), rather around the centre point – it is the precise distances involved here that are important.

Negotiation rarely comes out of the blue. There is usually a history of contact between the two parties, which may include written contact such as correspondence, or earlier meetings. Whether extensive or minimal such initial communication sets the scene and to some extent provides the agenda.

Negotiation needs an agenda. It may be useful to recap, to refer to the case so far, to any agreements made or indications given, or to whatever history may be useful or necessary. Persuasion precedes negotiation, so if the first contacts were concerned with a more fundamental agreement, and a case had to be accepted before terms and conditions could be debated, then it may be necessary to refer to this.

The initial stance

This refers to the starting point that each party goes for. Some judgement is necessary in choosing this, as the right starting point can facilitate the moves you want to make thereafter. There are many options; two follow.

■ *Going for the quick kill*. At one end of the scale you can go for what is described as the quick kill. 'Here are my conditions, take them or leave them.' Such an approach does not, in fact, rule out negotiation. It simply starts by making it clear a hard approach is being taken and little will be given away. Working from a powerful position, this – or something well to one end – may be an appropriate starting point. It is often used in wage bargaining. But even though it implies strength it must allow for some change or it risks being rejected out of hand.

Take care. The ritual is important and if people expect some movement this approach may stretch their credibility.

■ *Taking a softer approach*. At the other end of the scale, or towards it, the conversation might start on a different note, something like: 'Let's talk about what you want. We are reasonable people and want to secure agreement.' This may be more suitable when you do not have such a clearly strong case, but go too far with it and it will create, or increase, dis-advantage.

It is sometimes said that the higher the opening bid (initial stance), the better the final deal achieved by whoever makes it. Certainly it is difficult to negotiate down from nothing, and an initially exaggerated stance can pull the other party off balance and change their perception about the kind of deal that might be struck. This can mean that the first phase of negotiation is only a clarification of initial stances. A better, less extreme, point is then adopted by each party. Then negotiation really gets under way.

Building bridges to agreement

Consider what is going on as the negotiation commences. On the one hand taking initial stances distances participants, like two knights taking up positions on opposite hill tops prior to meeting to do battle in the valley between.

On the other hand, and because of this, there is a need to build **bridges of rapport**. These are inserted to bring the parties together – or at least closer together – in a way that prompts discussion and sets the scene for what needs to be achieved. Each party will introduce bridges that help their own case.

The other party is more likely to see your point of view if they can relate to your position and circumstance. Bridges make this more likely. There are many approaches:

- Open the discussions on a neutral subject to allay any hostility, obtain some initial agreement and get the other person talking.

- When holding back, give assurance that you will make every effort to come to a mutually agreeable outcome.

- Demonstrate respect for both the other party and the process you are embarking on; for example, compliment them about something already done that helps the process.

- Refer back to past agreement; this reinforces persuasion.

■ Present some of the values to your offering, even if you plan to negotiate them out later.

■ Be clear about complex issues.

All such tactics put the conversation on a basis of sweet reason. Even attempts to get the other party's list of requirements on the table can be undertaken in away that seems helpful: take an interest in them, their needs and views. This combines a show of genuine concern with something that, in fact, strengthens your position.

Keep finding out

Ask questions, and listen – really listen – to the answers. Get the other parties' position clearly in mind. Information is power in negotiation, and while you do not want to make people feel they are undergoing the Spanish Inquisition, the more you discover the better. Try to strike the right balance. We return to questioning techniques later.

Starting to trade

Trading concessions may well start at this stage. Even if they initially reflect peripheral issues, it can still set the scene for what follows. Avoid giving anything away early on. Even saying, 'Why don't we talk this through over lunch – my treat', may give the wrong impression. Better to say, 'If you agree to finalise matters today, then I will buy us lunch and we can chat this through in comfort.' If this kind of swap is handled informally, then no one need feel boxed in. The conversation can move naturally to a more business-like level. Then the trading can really start.

Trading concessions: the rules

Trading can take the form of tentative exploration, as in the example above on a 'if . . . then . . .' basis. Alternatively, it may take on a more demanding tone. In either case two important overall rules apply at this stage.

Rule 1: never give a concession – trade it reluctantly

The first part ('never give') is important because the number of variables is finite and you want your share. The second is important too, because perception is as important to how things go as fact. You want to be seen to be driving a hard bargain, otherwise you may not be taken seriously.

Rule 2: optimise or minimise every concession

This means optimising your concessions and minimising theirs. You can do this in terms of both value and how you talk about them. Try to build up the value, significance and importance of anything you offer and minimise what is offered to you.

The two sides of this process are worth exploring.

- **Optimising your concessions**. This means:
  - stressing the cost (financial or otherwise) to you: 'Well, I could do that but it will involve me in a lot more work'
  - exaggerating, but maintaining credibility – do not overstate and, if possible, provide evidence: 'Well, I could do that but it will involve me in at least twice as much work. I have just been through . . .'

- referring to a major problem which your concession will solve. 'I suppose, if I was to agree that, it would remove the need for you to . . .'
- implying that you are making an exceptional concession – 'I would never normally do this, but . . .'

Another approach, suitable for someone you have met before is
- referring to past discussions, and their successful outcome, and what you did for them. 'Remember how useful so and so was? I suppose we could go down that route again, how about . . .'

Such lead-ins not only build the significance of what you are offering, and make it more acceptable, but also make it more likely to be accepted quickly because there is an implied urgency. This is something that you may elect to exaggerate where appropriate.

- **Minimising their concessions**. Even if you plan to accept the concessions this means:
  - not overdoing the thanks – not a profuse 'thank you so much', but a brief, even dismissive 'thanks'. This is as much a matter of tone as of the words used
  - depreciating them, belittling the value: 'Right, that's a small step forward, I guess'
  - amortising them where appropriate – that is, divide them where smaller units will sound less impressive. 'Well, at least that would save me X every month', rather than quoting the annual figure
  - treating them as given and thus of no real value; a brief acknowledgement may be all that is necessary to give this impression: 'Right, let's do it that way'
  - taking it for granted, in fact saying it is not a concession at all but a foregone conclusion: 'Fine, I was certainly assuming that . . .'
  - devaluing by implying you already have what is being offered; 'OK, though I already have '
  - accepting, but in doing so implying that you are doing

a favour: 'I don't really need that, but fine, let's arrange things that way if it helps'

- linking value to time, implying it is now not worth what is implied: 'Well, that helps a little, but it isn't of major importance now we have . . .'
- denying any value: 'That really doesn't help.'

Minimising concessions does not work in every environment. In the Middle East, for example, the reverse is necessary. Always check local conditions if you have to work overseas, and in any case you should use factors like exaggeration carefully.

As concessions are either minimised or optimised as appropriate, the skilled negotiator trades a concession which in fact costs them little. It has, though, an implied value which brings a relatively more valuable concession in return from the other side.

It is this difference in value that gives an edge. A concession which you offer, but which you imply is of little or no value, is likely to prompt the offer of a low-value concession in return. Thus throughout the process you must play down your thanks for concessions gained and imply their low value, and build up the value of everything that you may concede. The only restraint on this exaggeration is the need to retain credibility with the other person.

It is all a question of degree. People know there is a ritual to negotiation, but still have to form a judgement of how far this goes.

There can be a large number of balls in the air during negotiation. Keeping track of the variables is quite a task, but you can prepare for it. If you have thought through what you want to do, considered the possibilities and anticipated the reaction of the other side, then you will have a picture that you can amend and adapt as discussions proceed. It may help to imagine the variables as boxes of different weights.

The dangers here are very real. If you forget something, or don't deal with it appropriately and at the right time, it may be impossible to bring it up later, or from a strong position. Make sure you have the overall position clearly in mind as you deal with the various points. If you are organised then anyone less so is at a disadvantage in dealing with you, so this can produce another edge.

IN SUMMARY

■ Consider and organise what will give you power in discussion and deal with this as part of your preparation.

■ Always remember that variables are the core of the process.

■ Use the four key tactical principles in every negotiation.

■ Trade variables and make your description of them — those given or received — enhance your case.

3 · Using Techniques to Keep Ahead

Individual techniques must be selected and deployed in a way that strengthens the whole approach.

In this Chapter:

1 TEN KEY TECHNIQUES

2 USING THE TECHNIQUES

3 BEING IN CHARGE

Knowing, and then using appropriately, the various techniques that can be deployed to strengthen a negotiation meeting; ten key techniques are described to illustrate the principle.

With the rules set out so far in mind, in this chapter we review some other techniques to make your negotiating work effectively. The following ten key ideas are in some ways basic, but all are useful techniques and begin to demonstrate the process at work.

1. TEN KEY TECHNIQUES

Using silence

Saying nothing can sometimes be as powerful as speaking, providing silence is used at the right time and in the right way. As most people begin to feel embarrassed by a silence, after even a few seconds, it can take a conscious effort to hold it, but it can be worthwhile.

In trading concessions, if you cannot optimise or minimise, then silence can imply that you are non-committal.

Being silent can imply certainty on your part, and thus uncertainty in another. Having made a clear suggestion – you wait. You will find it's not so difficult to ensure the other person speaks first. Maybe they need to think about it. If you chip in prematurely you may find yourself diluting your case unnecessarily.

Consider an example. A company buyer was speaking on the telephone to a potential supplier and, with a good quote in front of him, challenging the price without really saying anything very clearly: 'I am still a bit concerned about the price.' The supplier defended the deal as being good, which it was. He asked if it did not seem reasonable to the buyer, who said nothing at all. Embarrassed, the supplier started to justify the figures and again ended with a question that was ignored.

After three silences which the supplier found awkward, he said 'Would another five per cent get the order?'

A silence can be powerful, and, if it is not coped with well by the other party, is an easy technique with which to win points.

It may seem silly initially, but it is useful to count (silently in your head) if you want to hold a silence, because what seems like a terrible gulf of silence is often in fact just a few seconds.

Summarising frequently

By definition, negotiations can often be complex. They involve juggling a number of variables. It is easy to lose the thread. Never be afraid to summarise — recapitulate where you have got to so far, how one aspect of the discussion has been left. Linking this to using 'suppose' or 'what if. . .?' keeps the conversation organised and allows you to explore possibilities without committing yourself until you are ready. You might make this sort of comment: 'Right, we have agreed that we need to sort cost, delivery and timing. Now if we take . . ., then . . .'.

Making notes

This too helps keep complex negotiations on track. While certain meetings are too informal for full note-taking to be appropriate, even a few words noted down can help. Never leave yourself groping for what was said. Not only will the lack of recall worry you, but the fact that you are needing to ask calls your expertise into question and may spur the other party on to try harder.

Not only will taking notes prevent you being caught out over something factual, but making them or checking them can have another advantage. It gives you time to think. As you say 'Let me just note that down', or as you check 'Let me just see what we agreed about that,' you can be thinking. The brain works faster than the pen. It is surprising how much thinking you can do as you write two or three (sometimes irrelevant!) words on your pad.

> *You do not need to apologise for making notes (though it is sometimes courteous to ask permission to do so); being seen to do it shows you are concentrating.*

Leaving people feeling each step is good

Negotiation typically builds agreement progressively. Make sure you emphasise that each stage is good – preferably for both parties, but particularly for the other party – as you proceed. Phrases like 'that's a good arrangement', 'that will work well', 'that's fair', 'that's a good suggestion', help build the positive feeling that can lead to agreement.

Reading between the lines

Remember that negotiation is essentially an adversarial process. Both parties want the best for themselves, and the only signs of any approaching traps come via the other person, as do signs of success round the corner. Watch particularly for danger phrases that often mean something other than they seem to, even the very opposite.

Sometimes you may just want to take note of what you interpret in this way, sometimes you want to voice your understanding.

For example:

- 'You're a reasonable fellow.' Meaning: 'I am'.

- 'That's much fairer for both of us.' Meaning: 'Especially for me'. . . 'It looks like we are about there.' Meaning: 'There is something else I want'.

- 'All that's left is to sort out a couple of minor details.' Minor? For whom?

- 'That's all, then.' Followed by: 'But there is just one more thing . . .'

We return to this concept later.

Remaining neutral

Maintain neutrality as much and as long as possible. Negotiation works best as a balancing exercise. If you throw the whole basis of discussion up in the air – 'It is not as good as the other deal I am considering' – you risk taking everything back to square one. You may want to go back if you are not happy with the offer or the terms and conditions, but if you do you may risk returning to another process, that of persuasive communication.

Concentrating – all the time

Concentrate. Build in time to think if necessary. The power of silence has been mentioned; use it to think ahead. Use any delaying tactic to stop getting into difficulty, and always engage the brain before the mouth. Use a calculator, make a telephone call or just say 'Let me think about that for a moment', but give yourself pause for thought. On the other hand, if you can make the other party leap before they look, so much the better.

Keeping your powder dry

Beware of acting precipitately. Try not to make an offer, certainly not a final offer, until everything that needs negotiating is on the table. This may need no more than a question: 'Yes, I am sure I can help there, but is there anything else you want to consider?' You may need to probe to be sure of your ground before you proceed.

Beware of deadlines

It is said that there has not been a deadline in history that was not negotiable. Timing is a variable. How long will things take? When will they happen? All at once? Keep this in mind at all stages of the process.

Remembering constraints and variables are interchangeable

Almost anything the other side presents as fixed may be made into a variable. The word fixed is as likely to mean we do not want to negotiate this, as it cannot be used as a variable. It pays to act accordingly.

2 · USING THE TECHNIQUES

None of these points is, in itself, complex. They illustrate the multifaceted nature of negotiation, where a great deal is going on. Such techniques are useful; but none is a cure-all that will alone ensure the deal you want. The trick is in the overall orchestration of what you do.

3 · BEING IN CHARGE

Because of the need to orchestrate a complex process, it helps if you are in the driving seat. A line in Shakespeare's *Much Ado About Nothing* puts it well: 'When two men ride of a horse, one must ride behind.' Meetings, too, need someone in front. Taking a leading role does not have to mean it is a heavy one, indeed it may not even be obvious where direction originates.

*Run the conversation **you** want, in a way that **others** find they like, or at least find acceptable or professional.*

Getting off to a good start sets the process in train. Fine tuning as you go along keeps you progressing matters as you want. This means being extra-conscious of what the other person appears to be up to, and of how the interpersonal behaviour of the transaction is likely to work. It is to this that we turn in the next chapter.

IN SUMMARY

■ Review and decide the techniques of this sort that you might use and bear them in mind as you prepare.

■ Experiment and practise those you select to see what can become a permanent part of your armoury.

■ Use them as part of your overall management of the negotiating process.

4 · Refining Your Skills

The way people behave and how interpersonal behaviour can used is also important.

In this Chapter:

1 · ASKING QUESTIONS

It is difficult to find your way in the dark. Similarly it is difficult to negotiate without information. This applies to all sorts of things: the other person, their situation, their intentions and more. How do you discover such things? In a word – ask.

> *Given the adversarial nature of negotiation, a better analogy might be the difficulty of finding a lost black cat in a dark room – until it scratches you.*

Unless you know the facts, unless you know what people think and, most important of all, unless you know *why* things are as they are, taking the process on may be difficult or impossible. How do you communicate accurately and make negotiations go the way you want if you have little or no information? The answer in every such case might be stated as 'with difficulty'. Questions create involvement, they get people talking and the answers they prompt provide the foundation for much of what makes any kind of communication successful, especially a complex form like negotiation.

But questioning is more than just blurting out the first thing that comes to mind – *why do you say that?* – even a simple phrase may carry overtones and people wonder if you are suggesting they should not have said that, or if you see no relevance for the point made. In addition, many questions can easily be ambiguous. It is all too easy to ask something that, only because it is loosely phrased, prompts an unintended response. Ask 'How long will that take?' and the reply may simply be 'Not long'. Ask 'Will it be finished ahead of stage two commencing?' then the answer is more likely to help you and you are much more likely to be able to decide exactly what to do.

Beyond simple clarity you need to consider and use three distinctly different kinds of question:

- *Closed questions.* These prompt rapid 'Yes' or 'No' answers, and are useful both as a starting point (they can also be made easy to answer to help ease someone into the questioning process) and to gain rapid confirmation of something. Too many closed questions, on the other hand, create a virtual monologue in which the questioner seems to be doing most of the talking, and this can be annoying or unsatisfying to the other person.

■ *Open questions.* These cannot be answered with a simple 'Yes' or 'No' and typically begin with words like what, where, why, how, who and when, and phrases such as 'Tell me about . . .'. Such questions get people talking, they involve them and they like the feel they give to a conversation. By prompting a fuller answer and encouraging people to explain they also produce far more information than closed questions.

■ *Probing questions.* These are a series of linked questions designed to pursue a point: thus a second question that says: 'What else is important about . . .' or a phrase like 'Tell me more about . . .' gets people to fill out a picture and can thus produce both more detail and the 'why' which lies beyond more superficial answers.

It is important to give sufficient time to the process when finding out is necessary. It may also be important to give the clear impression to people that sufficient time *is* being given to something. This may indicate, say, the importance with which something is regarded; and the reverse may give the wrong impression – say of lack of concern. Both may be important. This is something that it may sometimes be useful to spell out: 'I think we should to go through this thoroughly, let's take a few minutes now and if that proves inadequate we can come back to it. Let's see how we get on'.

Information really is power, the more you know the easier it is to decide how to proceed, so this aspect of the process really does help you achieve an edge.

2 · LISTENING

Asking things is one thing. Listening is something else. Everyone appreciates a good listener. Negotiators need to be good listeners – the dangers of proceeding on assumptions, inaccurate information, or a lack of it, should be clear to us all. It is partly a matter of courtesy and partly a matter of credibility – you will never be felt to be taking something seriously if you appear unwilling to listen.

The need here is to really work at listening. The following list (reproduced from my book *Communicating with Your Staff*, Orion) sets out the essentials. You must:

- *want to listen* – this is easy once you realise how useful it is to the communication process

- *look like a good listener* – people will appreciate it and if they see they have your attention feedback will be more forth-coming

- *understand* – it is not just the words but the meaning that lies behind them you must note

- *react* – let people see that you have heard, understood and are interested. Nods, small gestures and signs and comments will encourage the other person's confidence and participation

- *stop talking* – other than small acknowledgements, you cannot talk and listen at the same time; do not interrupt

- *use empathy* – put yourself in the other person's shoes and make sure you really appreciate their point of view

- *check* – if necessary, ask questions promptly to clarify matters as the conversation proceeds; an understanding based even partly on guesses or assumptions is dangerous. But ask questions diplomatically, do not say 'You didn't explain that properly'

- *remain unemotional* – too much thinking ahead – *however can I overcome that point?* – can distract you

- *concentrate* – allow nothing to distract you

- *look at the other person* – nothing is read more rapidly as lack of interest than an inadequate focus of attention

- *note particularly key points* – edit what you hear so that you can better retain key points manageably

- *avoid personalities* – do not let your view of a another person distract you from the message

- *do not lose yourself in subsequent arguments* – some thinking ahead may be useful; too much and you suddenly may find you have missed something

- *avoid negatives* – to begin with clear signs of disagreement (even a dismissive look) can make the other person clam up and destroy the dialogue

- *make notes* – do not trust your memory, and if it is polite to do so, ask permission before writing their comments down

Many problems of communication are due to people not listening. It is always important, especially in a complex interaction such as negotiation. It is easy to be distracted, and you need to concentrate. Daydreaming, however constructively, is all too easy. Give the other party your undivided attention.

Another distraction is emotion. As the other person's argument unfolds you perhaps begin to feel anxious, or become angry.

> *Sometimes a display of anger may help, but it is rare for this to be appropriate and its use demands care and control.*

If such resentment takes over and prevents you listening your case will suffer. You may want to keep your first reactions hidden. It can be difficult to refer back, saying that something is a minor difficulty if when it was raised your face registered total dismay.

Check you have listened correctly. Never be afraid to interrupt a long speech to double-check you are following it. Ask for simplification or repetition if you wish. Beware too of hearing what you want to hear. Do not make assumptions, act on what the true message is. You may need to analyse the message as it proceeds and begin to form a response, but you have to keep listening as you do so if you are not to run into problems.

Finally, think about what will make listening easier. You cannot concentrate on what is being said if there is a lot of background noise, for example, an open-plan office, or if you are busy with something else as you talk, like driving a car. Try to pick a time when you are at your best, not over-tired or distracted by some personal emergency. When you pick up one hundred per cent of the message, you are in a much better position to respond effectively.

Listening successfully is a practical necessity if you are to excel at any communication situation including negotiation.

3 · READING BETWEEN THE LINES

Negotiation is not simply a matter of techniques, though these are important. It also depends on reading the behaviour of the other people who are involved in the process, and on you using behavioural factors yourself. Reading between the lines and acting accordingly is part of the negotiating ritual. To a degree this is a matter of experience, which needs time to accumulate. Nevertheless certain principles can be useful.

Negotiation has a language of its own. Some of it becomes ritual, adding nothing to persuasiveness and clearly part of the fabric rather than the content of what is being said. Some is a ploy, and we need to read between the lines to see what motivation lies behind the comment or phrase.

For instance, consider the hidden signals in the following examples:

One party says:	and means:
We would find it extremely difficult to meet that deadline.	*So, if we do meet it, it must be worth something.*
Our organisation is not set up to cope with that.	*So, if we do, consider it a real favour.*
I do not have the authority to arrange.	*But someone else does.*
It is not our normal practice to do that.	*I could make an exception.*
I never negotiate on price.	*If you want to – you start.*
We can discuss that point.	*It is negotiable.*
We are not prepared to discuss that at this stage.	*But we will later.*
That's very much more than our budget.	*So it had better offer real value and extra benefit.*
It is not our policy to give additional discounts and if we did they would not be as much as ten per cent.	*Would you accept five per cent?*
Our price for that quantity is X.	*But for larger quantities . . .*
Those are the standard terms and conditions.	*But we could negotiate.*
It seems an extremely reasonable arrangement.	*It is best for me.*
It is a good price.	*It is profitable, for us.*
I can't say I am happy with the arrangement but . . .	*I agree, but may ask for something else.*

You will no doubt spot, or use in future, many more. The detail, and the nuances of everything said when negotiating, is very important. Does it mean what it seems? Can we check? Is it a ploy? Is it an opportunity? How can we gain an edge with a word or phrase?

It is wise to be constantly watchful, to take nothing at face value. Remember that when you use phrases with nuances they help you; if the other party uses them they may be warning signs, and potentially put you at a disadvantage. Recognising them, and their potential danger, is the first step to overcoming them if they are deployed against you.

Negotiation is an inherently fragile process. Details matter here and one phrase used rather than another or one phrase giving a warning sign missed may make a significant difference to your position.

4 · USING BEHAVIOURAL TECHNIQUES

A number of factors are important here, the following are key and act as examples:

■ **Keeping the temperature under control.** You negotiate best with a calm, considered approach. So does the other person. Whilst you do not want to make it easy for them, you do not want the fabric of negotiation to collapse either. Any behaviour you use must help your cause without demolishing the process. It is easy to get into a position where pursuing your cause does more harm than good. For instance, if you labour an issue on which agreement is difficult and refuse to budge, particularly early in a discussion, you may create an impasse from which it is difficult for either party to retreat. You need to keep the range of issues in mind. If necessary leave a point on one side to return to later. Having agreed some of the issues, overall views change. With a deal now in prospect the early sticking point may not seem so important and can be dealt with without real difficulty.

■ **Using hidden motives.** Icebergs are a danger to shipping not so much because of what can be seen of them, but because of what cannot. The iceberg concept can apply to discussion and negotiation. You ask something and do not seem to get a straight answer. The other party's suspicion may prevent it; they are so busy looking for hidden motives that they hinder agreement for no good reason. It makes sense to spell out why you are doing things, asking a certain question, pursuing a certain line so that at least most of what is hidden becomes clear. Of course, you may have motives you want hidden, at least for the moment, but it will not help if the other person thinks you are being several times more devious than you are.

■ **Flagging.** Clear flagging, or signposting, of how you are proceeding can help. Sometimes it just makes clear what you are doing: 'May I ask . . . ?' or 'Perhaps I might suggest . . . ?' At other times a specific reason makes getting what we want more likely: 'I think it might be easier to settle other details if we can agree a fixed budget first.' It is seen as a constructive step forward. On the other hand we should never flag disagreement. This is something to watch, as the natural response is to flag it instantly. Consider what happens in a simple example.

> *Such signposting cannot be overdone, and it can flag both conent (what you want to deal with next) and the nature of what is coming (for example, here in print, phrases like 'For example' are signposts).*

For example: to encourage constructive listening, A makes a suggestion: 'Perhaps we can aim for completion of stage one by Friday week'. B immediately disagrees: 'No, I think that's far too long'. Even if he goes on to explain why, and even if he is right, A is busy developing a retaliatory response from the moment he hears the word no. He does not listen to the explanation of why, and even if he half hears it, is already committed to his riposte.

People are more likely to listen constructively, and accept reasons, if they are given before disagreement is flagged.

Thus, if A makes his point, B might respond: 'That would be ideal. However, we agreed that the whole project should be finished by the end of the month. Does Friday week leave sufficient time for everything else?' There is much more chance that this will prompt thought and discussion, that a compromise can be found or a counter-suggestion accepted.

- **Summarising progress.** Good negotiators summarise regularly; many negotiations get complex and discussions can last awhile. Summarising can:
  - test progress and allow you to rephrase things said by the other party
  - help you gain the initiative in the discussion, or maintain the dialogue
  - ensure that both parties have similar interpretations of what is said, and thus avoid misunderstanding and subsequent acrimony

– not least, summarising acts as a mental organiser for you, helping you keep track of progress to date.

■ **Attacking psychologically.** Some things are said not as part of any argument but to put the other party at a psychological disadvantage; just to rattle them, and perhaps make them easier to deal with as a result. This might be because you blind them to something you do or because they are concentrating less and are therefore less adept at something they want to do. Either way there is merit in getting the other person to drop their guard as it were. Some such comments may be based on issues which are part of the discussion, such as pressure on timing and deadlines. Others may be solely cosmetic, like the elaborate lighting of a pipe or a pause to make an urgent telephone call in order to create a long silence or pause, during which you are thinking and they are sweating. All sorts of things can be used in this way, amongst them:

– playing for time: working something out on a calculator or making a phone call

– a smoke screen of demands, only one of which is important

- flattery or coercion
- an angry outburst or show of emotion
- apparent total fluency with the facts: wondrous mental arithmetic may have been worked out beforehand, or just be a guess which is said with sufficient confidence to sound authoritative
- physical arrangements: an uncomfortable chair or position, balancing a coffee cup and trying to take notes
- financial restraints made to seem irreversible
- pretended misunderstanding.

■ **Avoiding defend/attack spirals.** Because people feel it is not proper to hit someone without warning, disagreement often starts from mild beginnings. Whilst one party says 'I am not sure about this', or 'I think we should aim for better than that', gently moving towards a major negative, the other senses what is happening and begins to prepare a counter-argument. Good negotiators do not put the other party on their guard, and effectively provide time for them to react well. If it is appropriate to attack then they do so without warning.

■ **Proposing counter suggestions**. Suppose you make proposal X and then the other person makes proposal Y. If you automatically think they are disagreeing, you will not be receptive and may not consider the alternative properly. If so your riposte can lead into a series of monologues, with both sides seeing the other as unhelpful and unconstructive. Progress is blocked when proposal X and Y are not really so far apart, and things could be moving together. This needs careful judgement.

■ **Avoiding deadlock.** The purpose of negotiation is to make a deal. Deadlock does nothing for either party. The search for variables has to go on until a deal is possible. It is usually only a question of time. However, if there are moments of deadlock it is helpful to think of the conversation flowing like a stream, which will always find a path round obstructions rather than through them. Never underestimate the chances of a new path, nor over-estimate your opponent's power and determination to remain unmoving. Try to find out why there is deadlock, and search widely for concessions or variables that will break it. In dire cases suggest a break, agreeing as much as possible before it, or even the involvement of other people. Try anything to create a real shift in what is happening.

■ **Using ritual approaches.** In certain parts of the world it is necessary to bargain in the shops and markets, not simply to secure a good price but to win respect. The process itself is important, not just the outcome. This is true of any negotiating situation. Some professional negotiators, who enjoy the game, feel frustrated if agreement is too quick or too simple. Negotiation must be allowed to take its course, and they will put up more and more conditions or elements to keep the process going. In such circumstances it may be wise never to make the first offer, not to make unacceptable conditions or drive impossible bargains.

As an example of this: remember particular traditions. A man visiting Hong Kong for the first time wishes to buy a watch. He had been told about the bargaining, and the percentage drop in price for which he should aim. He set off round the shops and, despite his best efforts, could get only half-way towards the suggested discount. Back at the hotel, discussing this with a local colleague, he asked what was he doing wrong. 'How long were you in each shop?' asked the colleague. On hearing that it was ten minutes or so, he suggested the visitor try again and give it half an hour.

The newcomer then discovered that only after twenty minutes or so, when you were sitting on a stool and coffee had been produced, did the bargaining get serious. Next time he came out with a nice watch and a good deal, and a little more understanding about the psychology of negotiation.

There are limits of course, but if the other party wants to take their time, let them. It may be worth it in the end. Timing is an important factor, and has to be handled just right.

■ **Linking to future relationships.** Always aim to end on a pleasant note. Negotiation can get acrimonious, hard bargains are driven, but people need to work or play together again. It may be good for future relations for the last move to be towards the other party, maybe throwing in one last small sweetener as the final agreement is made. This can stand you in good stead next time round. With colleagues these may be a regular part of your work.

5 · READING PHYSICAL SIGNS

We have looked at reading between the lines of what is said, but words, tone and emphasis are not the only ways messages come over when we speak with someone. People project all sorts of non-verbal clues to their feelings. Body language is an inexact science, but interesting and worth some study. One gesture is not an infallible sign of anything. An unbuttoned jacket may only mean it is a tight fit; wearing a jacket at all may indicate fierce air conditioning rather than formality. However, the checklist that follows provides some guidelines to what may be indicated by what.

Your intention should be not to over-react to anything, or to use one gesture as an infallible sign, but not to ignore indications that could be useful either. Proceed with care.

It is worth keeping an eye on body language through the whole process of negotiation. Remember, though, that it is only providing clues and should not become a fixation. There are plenty of other things to concentrate on.

Again an example from a different culture makes a point regarding expected behaviour. A meeting is about to take place in Malaysia. A European visitor has had some correspondence with the general manager of a local organisation and a meeting is arranged. The European is greeted cordially, offered a drink and as the meeting seems about to get under way he is given a business card. He tucks it quickly in his top pocket and begins to state his case. A small point, but the ritual of business card exchange is an important one in the East. It is expected that you study a card, view it as important and store it safely. Certainly you need to hand over one of your own in exchange. Not doing so will not make the discussion collapse in ruins, but any apparent failure to understand local conditions might have a negative effect.

The moral: it pays to check such local differences of behaviour and social nuance.

> *It is not necessary to go overseas to find this sort of thing, just dealing with a kind of person with whom you are unfamiliar may necessitate similar care.*

It is one thing to check currency rates and tariffs, it is another to remember not to point your feet at someone in case it causes offence, as in Buddhist countries. Such examples make a general point which may stand further investigation if you plan to deal internationally.

The reason for being sensitive to what is said, nuances, gestures, etc is to help you stay in line with the two basic factors of negotiation: your plan and your reading of how things are going and being received.

Checklist
Body language clues

The checklist that follows is not intended as points cast in stone, more as guide to what *may* be indicated. The more signs point to the same thing the more certainly you might take on board the message, however caution is always wise and you should always bear in mind that, at best, body language offers clues not infallible insights.

- **Open mindedness** is shown by:
  - open hands
  - unbuttoned coat

- **Wariness** is shown by:
  - arms crossed on chest
  - legs over chair arm while seated
  - sitting in armless chair reversed
  - crossing legs

- fistlike gestures
- pointing index finger
- karate chops

■ **Thinking/analysing** is shown by:
- hand to face gestures
- head tilted
- stroking chin
- peering over glasses
- taking glasses off – cleaning
- glasses earpiece in mouth
- pipe smoker gestures
- getting up from table – walking
- putting hand to bridge of nose

■ **Confidence** is shown by:
- steepling of the hands
- hands on back of head – authority position
- back stiffened
- hands in coat pockets, with thumbs outside
- hands on lapels of coat

- **Territorial dominance** is shown by:
  - feet on desk
  - feet on chair
  - leaning against/touching object
  - placing object in a desired space
  - hands behind head – leaning back

- **Nervousness** is shown by:
  - clearing throat
  - whew sound
  - whistling
  - cigarette smokers
  - picking/pinching flesh
  - fidgeting in chair
  - hands covering mouth while speaking
  - not looking at the other person
  - tugging at trousers or skirt while seated
  - jingling money in pockets
  - tugging at ear
  - perspiration/wringing of hands

- **Frustration** is shown by:
  - short breaths
  - tutting sound
  - tightly clenched hands
  - wringing hands
  - fistlike gestures
  - pointing index finger
  - running hand through hair
  - rubbing back of neck

- **Boredom** is shown by:
  - doodling
  - drumming
  - legs crossed – foot kicking
  - head in palms of hands
  - blank stare

- **Acceptance** is shown by:
  - hand to chest
  - open arms and hands
  - touching gestures

- moving closer to another
- preening

■ **Expectancy** is shown by:
- rubbing palms
- jingling money
- crossed fingers
- moving closer

■ **Suspicion** is shown by:
- not looking at you
- arms crossed
- moving away from you
- silhouette body towards you
- sideways glance
- touch/rub nose
- rubbing eye(s)
- buttoning coat
- drawing away

- **Alertness/attention** is shown by:
  - hands on hips
  - hands on mid-thigh when seated
  - sitting on edge of chair
  - arms spread, gripping edge of table/desk
  - moving closer
  - open hands
  - hand to face gestures
  - unbuttoning coat
  - tilted head

Body language is something worth keeping an eye on through the whole process of customer contact.

Remember though that it is only providing clues, a few pieces of the jigsaw, perhaps, and should not become a fixation. After all, there are plenty of other things to concentrate on.

6 · REACTING TO OTHER PEOPLE'S TACTICS

Negotiation demands constant fine-tuning. Just as in a sailing boat a hand needs to be kept on the tiller to compensate for wind and tide and maintain smooth progress towards a destination, so it is with negotiation. However well planned your tactics, you are constantly having to respond to the other party. Sometimes this means dealing with something you expected, at least at some point and in some form, and which you can be prepared for. On other occasions it means responding quickly to unexpected things.

The overall objective is to remain on course. You are heading towards your objectives whatever happens, though there may need to be some give and take. It is important that any response you make is, whilst prompt, also considered. Some of this can only come with practice; it is always worth analysing what went well, less well and what there is to learn from a negotiation, whatever the outcome.

The following examples may help accelerate experience. They indicate some of the tactics you may face and suggests what the other party hopes for as a result, and your possible response.

- *Other party's behaviour:* **chaos**: displays anger, storms out, takes umbrage.
  - *Hoping you will:* apologise, give concession, or get angry yourself.
  - *Your action:* keep calm, express your concern at any misunderstanding, seek clarification, let things return to normal before trying to proceed.

- *Other party's behaviour:* **poor me**: plea for special sympathy, concern or approach because of their situation.
  - *Hoping you will:* give more because you feel sorry for them.
  - *Your action:* do not be put off or be overly sympathetic, acknowledge the problem, restate your position and take the conversation back on track.

■ *Other party's behaviour:* **not me**: claims they cannot make decision, must refer to boss, spouse, committee.
  - *Hoping you will:* yield to pressure without souring relations: it is not my fault.
  - *Your action:* ask questions to ascertain whether it is true or just a ploy. In some meetings it may be worth checking early on whether they have the authority to make an arrangement.

■ *Other party's behaviour:* **only option**: keeps suggesting unacceptable option, without alternative.
  - *Hoping you will:* be forced into agreement, seeing no option.
  - *Your action:* keep calm, bear your objectives firmly in mind, suggest other alternatives such as a middle ground, keep setting out the problem.

■ *Other party's behaviour:* **no way**: immediately stating one element as non-negotiable.
  - *Hoping you will:* give up or offer a great deal to try to make it negotiable.

- *Your action*: offer to set that element aside, moving on to other things and getting back to it once rapport is established and agreement is clear on some other elements.

■ *Other party's behaviour:* **what**?: overreaction to something, shock-horror to indicate impasse.
  - *Hoping you will:* offer a rapid concession to compensate.
  - *Your action:* ignore the first response and restate the issue to prompt a more considered, informative response.

■ *Other party's behaviour:* **can't**: opens with a problem, we can't do anything unless the project can be completed by the end of the month.
  - *Hoping you will:* concede.
  - *Your action:* question for truth – it is more likely an initial stance – refer to the other variables.

■ *Other party's behaviour:* **no-can-do**: contains no detail or reason but is very negative: 'That's just not at all acceptable'.
- *Hoping you will:* see it as intractable and give in.
- *Your action*: ask for detail, why it is unacceptable, how different it needs to be; get away from the unspecific and down to the facts.

■ *Other party's behaviour:* **something more**: an overt request for some extra benefit.
- *Hoping you will:* give it to gain goodwill and keep things going.
- *Your action:* investigate the trading possibilities; if I give you X, would you be able to agree to Y?

■ *Other party's behaviour:* **policy**: the rules are quoted; 'more than my job's worth' e.g. company policy.
- *Hoping you will:* read it as unchangeable and not even try to negotiate.
- *Your action:* check whether it is true, whether there are exceptions or others have authority to make them.

Rules are made to be broken but be prepared for this to be difficult on occasion and, if necessary, to leave it.

■ *Other party's behaviour:* **sell me**: negotiation is dependent on a tacit agreement, e.g. to buy, action. If the deal is put in question the whole situation may be changing.
  – *Hoping you will:* give in to secure agreement.
  – *Your action:* ask questions, do we go back to the stage of persuasion, or is it a ploy? If so stick to your position and push back hard.

■ *Other party's behaviour:* **big vs**. **little**: a big deal is made of a small point, then used as a concession for something they really want.
  – *Hoping you will:* see the first as a real issue and trade, in away that is not a good exchange.
  – *Your action:* check real importance, compare and deal with the two things together.

■ *Other party's behaviour:* **no progress**: things appear to be dead-locked, no clear way out.

- *Hoping you will:* give in as only way forward.
- *Your action:* suggest a real change, a break, or the introduction of an arbitrator; if it is a ploy these may be resisted and you can get back on track.

If you are a regular negotiator it may be worth keeping notes of your own examples, as an aide memoire for the future.

Getting results

There are several aspects to negotiation. The process itself is important, the structure and sequence of events contribute to its success. The ritual may be important, the techniques certainly are, but it is ultimately people that make it work, so no aspect of interpersonal behaviour must be overlooked.

Any difficulty is likely to be less because the individual elements are themselves complex, than because of the problem of orchestrating the whole thing. Those who get every aspect moving together effectively are likely to make the best negotiators.

IN SUMMARY

■ Remember information is a major asset in negotiating. Ask — check if you are not clear — ask some more, but act on the basis of a good understanding of the situation.

■ Listen and note information so that it can be retained and used at will.

■ Do not take what is said at face value — read between the lines.

■ Observe peoples' stance, manner and body language as part of the available feedback, assess what you see, but do not ignore clear signs.

■ Use behavioural techniques yourself and respond to the behaviour of others in a considered fashion.

5 · Orchestrating the Process

Successful negotiation is not the result of some magic formula, it is created by making the whole process work for you.

In this Chapter:

The key issues that matter most are summarised in this chapter and cover both the overall principles and the tactics.

Negotiation is part art, part science. Going about it in the right way increases the likelihood of success. However, it does not guarantee it. It is a dynamic, interactive process. It needs to be conducted in a way that is well planned, yet flexible, that recognises that the people element is the most important – and the least predictable.

The danger with dissecting any such process is that it can then be difficult to put the pieces together. So, now it is time to pull together the essentials.

1 · ORCHESTRATING THE KEY ISSUES

To negotiate successfully you must see the process in the round, take a broad view and continue to do so throughout the process. This means you must have a good grasp of the principles involved, for it is that which allows you the opportunity to orchestrate and fine-tune the process as you proceed. Small adjustments as you progress can make all the difference.

Summarising the principles

1. *Definition*: negotiation is about bargaining to reach a mutually agreeable outcome. This is the win-win concept.

2. Never neglect your preparation. Have a clear plan but remain flexible.

3. Participants must regard each other as equals. Mutual respect is essential to both conduct and outcome.

4. There is a need to abide by the rules. Negotiation is about discussion, rather than debate. There is little place for overt oneupmanship or domination, yet each must fight their corner.

5. Put your cards on the table, at least on major issues. Do not pretend powers or state intentions that are untrue.

6. Patience is a key characteristic of the good negotiator. Take your time, do not rush discussion or decision making. Delay is better than a poor outcome.

7. Empathy is vital. Put yourself in the other's shoes, see things objectively from their point of view.

8. State clear objectives. Being open early on about overall intentions can save groping in the dark.

9. Avoid confrontation. Do not get into a corner you cannot get out of. Avoid rows and showdowns, but stand firm and keep calm.

10. Treat disagreement carefully. Act as devil's advocate, apparently looking at the case from the other's viewpoint, to avoid a confrontational 'I disagree' style.

11. Deal with concessions progressively. Where concessions have to be made, make them unwillingly and one at a time – and trade them.

12. Do not let perfection be the enemy of the good. An outcome that is one hundred per cent what you want is rarely an option. Be realistic, do not waste time and effort seeking something out of reach.

13. Use openness but not comprehensively. Declaring your plans and intentions may be useful to the discussion. You may want to keep hidden the motivation behind them.

14. Stick with your objectives. Set your sights high and settle as high as possible. Know when to drop the whole thing rather than agree a totally inappropriate deal.

15. Keep up your guard. Maintain your stamina, bide your time. The other party may persevere for hours to see when you will crack.

16. Remain professional. For example, respect confidences that are given in the course of negotiations. Such consideration builds relationships and may help you next time.

17. Never underestimate people. A velvet glove may be disguising an iron fist.

18. End positively. Neither party will get exactly what they want, but if the deal is agreeable emphasise this at the end.

All these points are surely uncontentious, but *all* must be borne in mind throughout the process.

> *One factor differentiating the most successful negotiators from others is that they keep a clear overview of what they are aiming to do throughout the process.*

Summarising the tactics

Like any interactive skill negotiating is dependent on a plethora of factors. The following are picked to provide a top ten of things likely to be most useful. You might like to compose your own list, see how it varies and make sure it reflects exactly the kind of negotiating you do and the kind of people it pits you against.

1. Select the right starting point. Your plan should make it easy for you to take the initiative and quickly get onto your agenda.

2. Aim high, then the trading moves you nearer what you regard as a good position.

3. Do not make your feelings obvious. There is an element of bluff. If your face and body language say 'this is minor' as you respond to something major you will do better.

4. Use silence. Some things demand no reaction at all.

5. Watch for early difficulty. Let a rapport and momentum build up before you tackle contentious issues.

6. Do not exaggerate facts. They can be verified and such exaggeration only causes problems later.

7. Communicate clearly. Remember the need for understanding as a foundation to the whole process.

8. Be seen to go with the other person's way of doing things, at least to some degree and particularly if you are on their ground.

9. Do not push too hard. There is usually a line beyond which the outcome is not a better deal, but complete breakdown.

10. When negotiation is finished, stop. Once agreement is reached, clear, agreed and perhaps noted, move on to other matters. Otherwise people say 'I have been thinking . . .' and you are back to square one.

The importance of different factors like these depends on the nature of a particular negotiation. Something full of complex financial details poses different problems from something simpler.

Whatever you do, you need to deploy appropriate techniques from the full range of possibilities, picking those most likely to suit the circumstances and making sure you can make them work.

2 · A FEW THINGS TO AVOID

What else helps? First – a few things to avoid. You will only excel if you never:

■ over-react if responses are negative; the other person is at pains not to say how excellent every point is

■ allow yourself to become over-emotional, unpleasant, provocative or insulting; a planned and controlled display of emotion may be useful, but you must know what you are doing

■ agree to something you do not want; in many situations there is a minimal deal which your plan should identify, below which it is better to walk away.

Every new situation is an opportunity to learn. Every negotiating situation can teach you something: what works well, what to avoid, what best fits your style. The detail is important. Sometimes what makes the difference between success and failure is small and seemingly insignificant. One phrase, even one gesture, may make such a difference. If all the details are right, the whole will be more likely to work well.

3 · PRODUCING REAL CLOUT

Negotiation is a topic about which no guide can be comprehensive. It is a dynamic, interactive process and even the best performance can be made more effective. The key things are to start, and ensure that the experience you gain makes what you do in future better and better.

Remember when you learnt to drive, or to juggle with flaming torches without burning holes in the carpet? You probably despaired of ever being able to concentrate on a disparate, and lengthy, list of things all at once, and make it work. Negotiation is no different. A basic shopping list of techniques will start you off and allow you to practise. Then with the basic techniques in mind you can add to your method of approach and continue to develop it.

Such conscious use of experience in the light of your awareness and knowledge of the process is the only way to develop real clout. You cannot expect that to come overnight, or without thought or practice.

4 · MAKING RESOLUTIONS FOR THE FUTURE

Finally, a few things are worth emphasising about this process of developing skills.

■ **Preparation is key.** Preparation really does make a significant difference. Yet it is so easy to miss out or skimp. Make
time for it, think about it, and everything else that follows will
be easier.

■ **Being aware of the process.** Secondly, try to develop a
consciousness of the process. If your mind is actively aware of
the overall issues, the complexities and the structure of what
is involved, rather than simply moving from point to point, the
whole process will be easier. This may seem difficult to begin
with. A chess player will concentrate on the current move in
the context of the next, the one after, and the opponent's response, all within an overall strategy; it is important in negotiation too. It does work and becomes easier with practice. In
time both the learning process and the deployment of the
many techniques will become a habit.

■ **Becoming confident.** Thirdly, remember that confidence
is paramount. Planning is the starting point for this. If you have
thought about both the principles and the detail of a particular
encounter, you will have more confidence in what you plan to

do. This will not only help you, it will be apparent to your opponent and you will come across in a way that will make the whole process easier.

We are, I hope, agreed that you can be a better negotiator if you work at it. Indeed, the process of trying will itself help you learn quicker and do better. Continue this process for a while and you will be a match for anyone.

Will you become a good negotiator? What you are able to do depends very much on how consciously you set about it. You need to understand and deploy the techniques appropriately. You also need confidence in your ability to do so effectively. Understanding, preparation, a considered approach — and practice — all build both technique *and* confidence.

Remember, good luck is what makes other people's negotiations successful. You are what makes yours succeed.

IN SUMMARY

At the end of a chapter that itself summarises the key
issues, perhaps two overall points can suffice to
conclude this review.

- Remember negotiation is an adversarial process. The
  other person is not 'on your side' as it were, and everything you do needs to respect this underlying fact.
  Quote: *When a man tells me he is going to put all
  his cards on the table, I always look up his sleeve.*
  (Lord Hore-Belisha)

- The most important factor in deciding the outcome of
  your negotiations is *you*. *What* you do and *how* you do
  it make all the difference, and how well you know the
  process and how well you prepare put yourself in a position to get the best possible deal will always influence
  the deal you get. As the old proverb says – *You don't
  get what you deserve, you get what you negotiate.*

It is precisely this principle that Annabel (quoted in the
Preface) seems to understand; and what makes her
likely to succeed.

Patrick Forsyth can be contacted at:

Touchstone Training & Consultancy
28 Saltcote Maltings
Maldon
Essex CM9 4QP
United Kingdom